ENTER: EXPLORING THE REALMS OF LIFE

ENTER: EXPLORING THE REALMS OF LIFE

Steve Girten

To order additional copies of this book, contact:
Xlibris
1-888-795-4274
www.Xlibris.com
Orders@Xlibris.com
781269

CONTENTS

About the Author

Enter: Exploring the Realms of Life is my second book. And I believe that I have learned a lot more about writing a book since the first one. I put more patience and thinking into *Enter*, trying to make it the best book that I can. For anyone who purchases this book, I really hope that you find it meaningful and interesting.

—Steve Girten

"The Meaning of Realm"

Kingdom, or area or range over within, where someone or something acts, exists, or has influence or significance; sphere; domain.

Social Workers, Caseworkers, RNs/CNAs - PRSC

Bed of pain and sorrows of only dreaming of a tomorrow. Knowing of the habits of morning and night, night to night. From dawning to realizing. To give, to take, forgetting how to hate. To put music to words and complete a new. To write to music for ideas.

Explaining what is known from the unknown. With a feeling understood in a movement by "being proud and confident." To watch and be watched, wondering and wondering, to hear the past through others' voices, stories, and memories seeming so vague.

—Steve Girten, Date Unknown

Eternity to the sea for the sky from the love we have inside. To feel and care, knowing you will always be there.

Heaven/Sleep/Faces

Serenity, contentment, vision of memory. Peaceful acceptance of truth and the ignorance of maturity that helps us sleep. And the pillow of faces of the past day that we remember.

The lies that ruin but the truths that gain in the long run and the secrets that keep us happy.

—Steve Girten, Date Unknown

Dreams We Share/Sleep If You Dare

Sun burning yet to the moonshine. Seeing in light people passing, pathway's pleased. Rest now. Sleep at ease.

Highway of rain, coming down on me.
The road so long, endless the sight of rain.
As fear sets in, uncertainty is known.
Is this our last love for another of whom we are with?
Trying to keep this love but of a scared hate that is felt.

The sun that we live for, the energy within us. Our eyes of perception that keep us going. And the freedom of the air.

—Steve Girten, Date Unknown

Golden Chain around His Neck, Symbol Shown as for Religion

Stolen soul walking on the street of a dark night. Lying under a bench, hiding from the sight of any person. Death like gliemes, view from the eyes, bones old and hard. The air that's felt not seeming the same.

Sounds of colors through the sky, neon lights from a rooftop, seeing bright. A kid lost on the street from arguments at home. Cold and sad he walks. People pass eyes meet. A feeling to grow as the warmth of understanding sets in.

—Steve Girten, Date Unknown

A Sense of the Night

To see what love can bring and what hate can do.

What do we want? The name that's not the same—individual and original. The name that's been given and the name that's been lived.

Awake, child of the night, haunted by light. Tight between your sheets, about to be welcomed to the streets. Dance, angel of darkness.

—Steve Girten, Date Unknown

Forests of insanity—the unlimited laughs and the eyes that look. Enchanted darkness, you can hear creatures in the mist of night. With the bright moon, you can see birds flying backward, silhouetted by the glow of the moon.

The love within caves, cities, mountains, and all the states. The discovery of the intangible world, that of beauty that is always there to find and/or share.

—Steve Girten, Date Unknown

My past keeps haunting me. The memories won't leave me alone. Is this destiny or just something I can't understand? Thinking of, wanting an idea to explain, something that won't stop. Like a flashback, it throws me off. Time, within timing, forgetting, knowing something is missing, something is not right. Now looking in the mirror, seeing something that's not clear, is it the tears or just some kind of fear? The tears are real; the rest just ain't true. As I remember saying bye to an average party at ways, things stopped a little, a bit slower, a bit sad and vague. The sad condition that's come over me, to be caught up within feelings of loss. But to be able to walk with confidence, of proper posture, of dress, with bold pride and eyes that stay focused. Like the sun of a new day, things have a way to pass and things that will have remained. With problems of life in general—job, career, family past, immediate family, and relatives.

The children and their lives and with the common situations of society, of the world. And all the money that can spread happiness. With all this, should we worry so much on things that don't seem right? But maybe it's the way toward freedom, finding the truth, fitting in with the flow—your flow within your life. In destiny, the things that attract, the things that fascinate, just the things that catch your eye. Stay focused, stay fair, and you will achieve your own destiny. And let it serve you.

—Steve Girten, December 23, 2010

We Are/We Were Still to Be/ Always We Will Be

The environment—the nature to see, the animals reflecting human life—and to relate to the needs of whoever deserves it. The fields with their plows and the woman that bows. The clouds in the blue sky and the eyes that see the beauty of nature and the eyes that witness the ones who cry.

—Steve Girten, Date Unknown

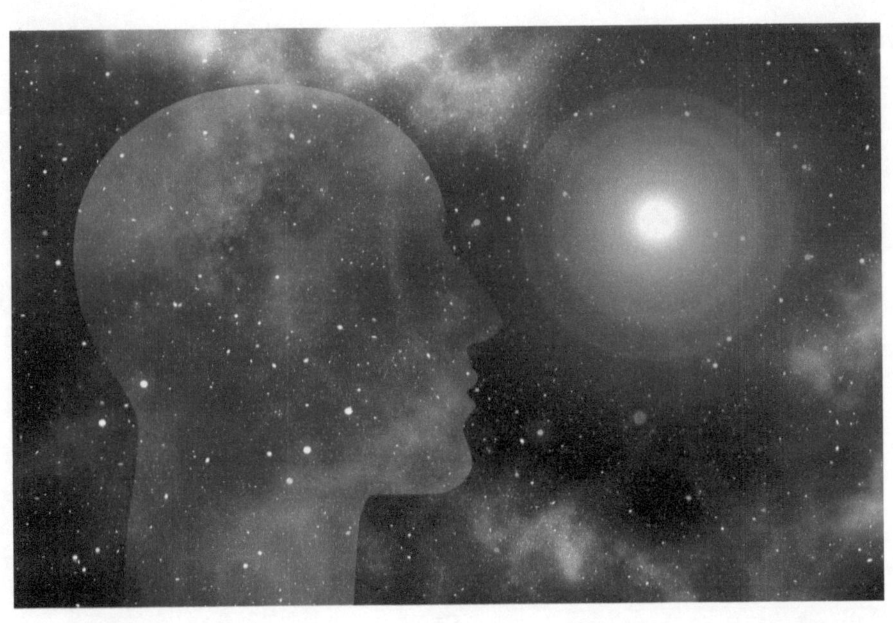

Minds of the ledgers—ten miles above, they reign with sight full power. "We stay, we listen, and we observe! The dead that really used their head!"

Discover heaven—land of the sky. Beginning ways—rhythms of the clouds and motions of nature. The earth originally was vacant, filled with water. But how the earth has changed. Now in 2018, the harmony of the universe is right here on Earth, joined with mankind's power of one.

Sun signs/moon signs
Sun shines/moon shines

—Steve Girten, Date Unknown

As the Mexicans get high and the whites watch, getting by, the world is moving and by the brightness of their eyes. Involve the sky, the ultimate way of being. The universe beyond immaculate power that we have never witnessed. Waterfall, waterfall, enlightenment of drowning, deep, deep into your mystical realm, falling, falling, memory flecting of cool wet—birth of conception. Knowing a way now to be brave, knowing to be saved and to use what's been given.

Noticing the scenery, recalling the recalled vague memory. Seeing something familiar, something known, and yet still unknown.

—Steve Girten, Date Unknown

Sea's in place, resurrection of spiritual life. To see where you're not to feel where you're not. The unbounded power of this connection. Has your world changed, and has it just begun?

Ceremony of prayers, with thinking through feelings, believing with faith, to help live.

I do; I see. But who does achieve? Is it the beautiful people, the ones who smile even when things aren't so good, the ones who make communication heard—accepted? No tomorrow's tears, your life that is there, your feelings that you should know. Is it the haunted, or the fear to live, or the worry of dying?

Vision in timing, rhyming in writing. The view, the point of God. The reality that hurts caused the condition/origin of nature. The involved religious belief and a want that may proceed, in all.

> Subtract death rate
> Increase birth rate

Ages of the past, matching the future of present date. The time's relating with subliminal meaning. The foreseen treating the past with magic. And the people talking, warning one another of a future to be.

—Steve Girten, Date Unknown

To plan, no past. To plan destiny—to give in with prayer, accept the time of reality, the being at your fullest.

Epic of an era, life goes on. But of the excitement that filled the air, with gold. What was sold, what was told. Dust to dust, the sunbeams and the chambers are ready. Objects—relics, gold. All around is intrigue, mystery—meaning of the marble door. Ancient place of deep religion, power, and meaning. The holiness that was filled is now a power of self-want of greed, all the visitors have despite all the Egyptian ways. The long-, long-lived days are gone. The temple of fear and of time is now.

—Steve Girten, Date Unknown

Some stranger unknown outside reason. Life alive, as in living. Fears alike, similar. Both striving for the same thing.

Clear but distant ideas—test the truth. With the mind itself doubting, believing. Looking for answers with the unknown.

Mirrors of fear—to see a face, a face you have never seen before, with the intent to find. Stranger to stranger, do I know you? To feel the other side and know you are still alive.

—Steve Girten, Date Unknown

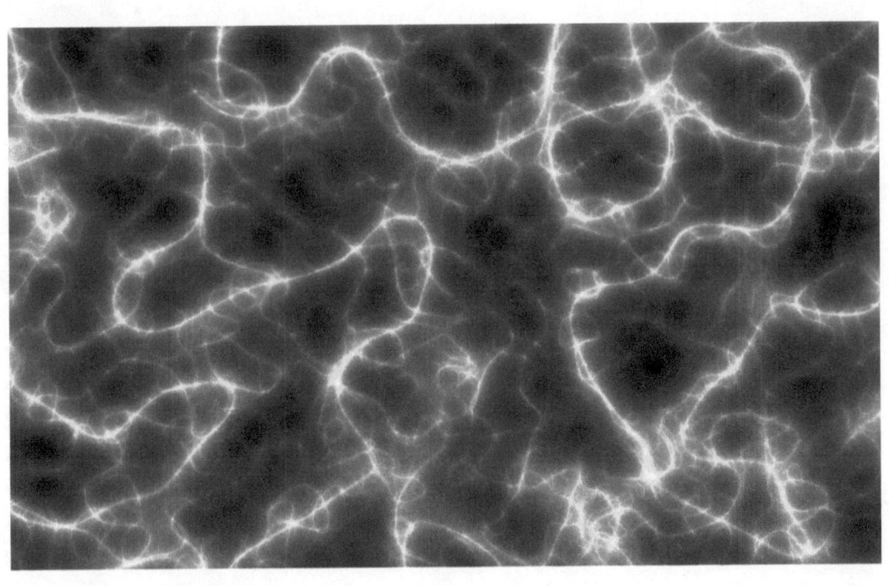

Sound of thunder with one star in the sky. Did someone die?
To see and to know something so unknown. With the ground
on fire and the grass wet from the morning dew.

The people who achieve, striving for beauty, perfection,
knowledge—the truths of life—and to really find love. Putting
your whole life into your passion. Life that's not there but the
feeling that is.

Steve Girten, Date Unknown

Being a movement maker, having power and control, with making decisions and deciding what is right. To try to understand things with compassion. The things that seem easy or great, or even wonderful, aren't always so true. There are sufferings, losses, laments, responsibilities, and heartaches. Regardless, to live your own life to the best and fullest of your abilities, that should be enough satisfaction to get you through.

Changes within the in between/beating death with every sign. Worried of tomorrow and worried of today. With life seeming to be passing away, but to explore the dreams that fantasize you, break away from all the ruins in life. Set your soul. Live on.

—Steve Girten, Date Unknown

Walking to the beach, the weather hot with a cool breeze. Wandering from neighborhood to neighborhood, losing track of time like in a dream—an unconscious state. And I walk to find water at a beach. With noting to have and nothing to do. I found the beach, people sitting on the rocks and families with their blanket's food and children looking all around. I searched for destiny out of a bottle, not knowing anyone and having nothing to lose. I soon found a new friend and a new bottle. As the sun set, I walked away with a smile. Now the sun was coming down, and I'm almost at home. The day I roamed, now feeling. At home, I sit on my bed, shoes slid off and eyes closed, jacket tossed to a near chair. Now my hair on the pillow, I sleep to another day.

—Steve Girten, Late 1900s

Girl—I see what she wears, the color of her hair, her sexy thighs, her blue eyes. Love comes into the room as she enters. Her shoes pink with white laces. As she approaches forward, straight as she walks, just seeing her face, wanting to kiss that face. Oh, her subtle lips. The light shining in her eyes, the look very clear. Dance of a dream to hold and feel her so near. Almost unreal—a touch of a lifetime.

"Sadness"

Like the rain, a feeling to be sad. But then to see you and be glad. Similar to a smile, similar to you. With a love so bright, just like the sun above. Sadness—to see you and then not to see you.

—Steve Girten, Late 1900s

Recently, I was worried, worried about being worried. Looking far away of living and of a good life. But cries, for nothing, and fears that aren't there. For you that is so near, stay away. I don't want your fears. To see without vision and to feel nothing near, to hear without words. And to yell and not be heard. Recently, I was worried . . .

Expression, glad—love in trust, the soft, gentle blessing of compassion.

My expression of dealing with a trusting love is sad and deeply hurtful. To feel the need of a companion, someone to share with. And hope of faith for a blessing, to live softly.

—Steve Girten, Late 1900s

My desert of magic, for you and me to let it be. We will carry rocks from the waters, we will hide our clothes in the sand, we will watch the tides, and we will choose our roles. Who we are and what we want to be. To dig holes to shelter the pain. To run, run in the rain. To get up to feel the same. We are here, nowhere else to be. Now is the time not to cry and be wrong from the fear.

To write about the sea and the sky, or even life. And what happens and of the feelings. To know love and beauty and describe it. To see more and explain it. Rhyming or not, to be able to sense more and write it. About anything!

—Steve Girten, Late 1900s

A whistle in the dark, music from a bar, faces seeing faces. The fear of love is close and near. A woman or a man, fight or just stand. To the car and have left the bar. All alone now, tonight was just right, so clear the fear, never so near. Feeling no pain as the sky begins to rain. And I am feeling the same.

The magic day—in the yard, a bench, and a neighbor friend. With one drum and two sticks. I soon set the drum between my legs. I hit the drum one stick at a time until I had a rhythm, rhythm with a smile and a laugh, knowing I did good and happy for the whole moment.

—Steve Girten, Late 1900s

Changes beyond belief, associating more with women and an outlook in a much better and positive way but of confidence and of surety. Adhering to the feeling to follow my soul for wisdom. But the awkward betrayal that scars life. The burden of responsibility to give more than live. The birth—love and religion—of freedom.

Imagine the sky, clouds way up high. Beyond the clouds and the sky is a feeling of content, of eyes closed, as like a numbing. With peace and happiness but the sorrow and fear. All around is given a love that is so near.

—Steve Girten, Date Unknown

To say you won with a loss. To know you're winning even when you're losing.

To refine the past, to make new things possible. To openly admit you need a change.

To be a kid, soft and innocent, young and very free. Wondering, wondering, wondering.

—Steve Girten, Date Unknown

The world we left so far behind. As we saw it, and as we remember it. Appearance of size, or is it hypnotized?

To see you shine brilliantly, brightly—beautiful is your complexion.

A heart sets accomplishment, to know what you want—and get it. And a smile that says it all. And love and joy for you forever and ever!

—Steve Girten, Date Unknown

"Systematic"

The sun and the moon. All planets in tune with the beautiful harmony of our universe. But so much is unseen.

—Steve Girten, February 3, 2017

Peaceful women's love, the pride of being a mother, and the pride of being a woman. Single, dating, or engaged—a woman's belief can go far.

Living I see you to understand the way of your life.

—Steve Girten, Date Unknown

I love you like a song
I hear you like a bird
I feel you like a heart
Never to part!

The erotic suggestion/temptation in the mansion of love.

Just to be brave enough to go inside that church that you have
seen from the outside so many times. With belief, the church
helps us remember.

The inner pain but with the strive to live life and the freedom
of not thinking.

—Steve Girten, Date Unknown

The sarcastic priest says, "Laughs are sad but needed." It's the cries that need attention. All the dead intentions that were never received. And all that love that should have been felt. And there's the baby's cry we hear in the dark—windy, night of distance. Then of a silence, the feeling of death, that creeps through the dark voids in power in intrigue and of bravery, just to seek the light and knowing of an awakening of new being—in desire and promises of truth. And of prayers but in a different form but to the belief of the same power.

—Steve Girten, June 28, 2017

Run and hide-and-seek and find, faster, faster as we ride. The car long and black, seating four. Of the beautiful scenery we explore.

Colors in the sky, will I see you when I die, will it take a lie or should I cry, or should I just fly? Colors in the sky is what I see up high, not just a cry or no lie, 'cause my love for you is way up high.

—Steve Girten, Date Unknown

Beyond death and the feelings of bounds. Structures seeming to be an illusion, new in this reality. Like the Indian's peace and the Egypt's mystery and power. Open is the sight of no fear around. Beautiful is the feeling; intriguing is the want.

—Steve Girten, Date Unknown

"Virtues"

A way of life
Complaining/happy
Who we like
Who we hate
And you we love
True sight
Passions
Integrity
Acceptance
Wisdom/knowledge
Brotherhood of belief
To rise above
Compassions of ways
Surrender/give
Class of money
Material want
Religion/knowledge
Peace within/peace shared
The sins/an adored love
Sex/guilt

—Steve Girten, Date Unknown

Materials of common. The art in which we show ourselves. The passion of appearance, such as painting, drawing, writing, singing, and even communicating.

The nation of life, the directions we take, and how we live it. All the cultures with their ways of living but of the stranger that is visiting to this unknown realm.

— Steve Girten, Date Unknown

Rain—memory: to describe rain as a feeling; maybe it brings sorrow. Maybe it's like joy. But with a misty night, a cigarette to light, night of delight. As the sun showers pour down, wet and us all around feeling the same.

Memory of to be hurt. The power from the past, from something that didn't last. With remembrance of scenes.

Behavior age - a learning stage.
Yes and no - the way to go.

—Steve Girten, Date Unknown

Help him find a way to pass the time of day. For he knows no limitations.

The young mind that deals with problems is a notice among his peers.

I am with you, through you, and about you.

To travel, to create, to experience—"acid."

—Steve Girten, Date Unknown

"Trying to Forget You Ever on My Mind"

Love relationship

My feelings for you are always the same.

In ways of feeling. Thoughts through time and motion. The longitude in life, the degrees of age. Woman in race, sexual pass. Oh, the outrageous taste!

"Oh, the Worried Mind!"

The sun, the world as we know it. And then the end, with a glow from the moon.

—Steve Girten, Date Unknown

The misty air, the lightly scented perfume. The night is ours, of boundless freedom—love in our air. The sights of color with structured objects, in balance within the area at being. We are right, they are wrong, but as we talk, as we get along.

The secret world, with glows from a spring, sparkled shiny eyes and skin of bronze. Love, like the soaring dove through the skies. Blue is the sky; love is the way.

—Steve Girten, Date Unknown

The path of freedom, the sight of destination. A journey of desires—to become divine. The seeker can travel through great imagination of dimensions—worlds of intrigue. All the pleasures of self-awareness. The perfection alely balanced, heart in the body and chemical structure. And of knowledge and the wisdom of age that can be acquired. The child with knowledge, wisdom of a sage. The universal love and the beauty of natural existence. And the vague idea of "God." In the twilight of the usually dark forest, there lies peace to be felt inside. In the deep ocean, when felt around, the mystery of death comes, that of fear, uncertainty. Of so deep, endless realms are felt. Late in unconsciousness, we see a vision of a palace. Now at midnight, the clock strikes. The sky beyond being our only salvation.

—Steve Girten, January 17, 2016

Lost in the wind like a bird, a bird in flight. My vision scattered and vague the sight with near areas surrounding. But of distance I see, to the unknown. So unsure, so confused. It's so magical; my perception grows. My focus of true amazement: the glittering sun. Has love finally come? It must before it's gone.

—Steve Girten, October 11, 2012

Forgetting the memory that can't be forgotten.

—Steve Girten, October 12, 2012

"Maybe a Song"

The human physical world unfolding, air—to reflect life. Let vision lead us.

Do you remember as young and free? Well, baby, that's the way it should be. Now with acquiring more age, to be satisfied you can be. And with your ears you can hear, and with your eyes, there is sight. Yeah, with a sense, you will know, you will feel, and you will grow. Loving of away—hey, hey.

—Steve Girten, October 9, 2012

Life is long, filled with tears. How I wish you were here. The struggle of attachment and the suffering to keep my love within. My love, the love I share not only inside but also of all around as it fits. Without any of us, without you, nothing would count!

—Steve Girten, October 11, 2012

My symbolic obsession with everything I see—and do. But for a great purpose and of a reason of meaning.

—Steve Girten, November 29, 2012

Family, unifying a life forced to get along, love that is still there. Being close, realizing the only way. Blood thicker than words, thicker than unknown knowledge.

Theory—divided, subjected ideal state deep within ourselves. As we see our life and all kinds of different lives, we must learn to appreciate and love the passing stranger.

—Steve Girten, Date Unknown

Virtue is knowledge—in the way we respect it. But the path of escaping and that realm inside your mind. With substances that enhance the head, a smell, a feeling, and a vision. The thin lines, the breaking points, and the barriers. The body like a shadow, with the glow of our soul inside. Bright the soul grows as light is filtered in.

—Steve Girten, Date Unknown

Ethics/beliefs trapped in existence.

"Schizophrenia"

The brain/the birth

—Steve Girten, Date Unknown

To see you, I need you. *Love*, can't live without you. The words you have said are so beautiful, so planned, so right and true. But hearing you and then seeing you, failures never to be appreciated. The near sight of your life in a light that reflects honesty, innocence, intelligence, compassion, and peace within your way. Your basic, subtle ways, with grace as you move, in a timing of brilliance of perfection.

—Steve Girten, December 4, 2011

With my ank around my neck and religion in my head, I see the sun seeming to always be new. And the love in people's eyes, not even a sigh. Bright and beautiful we share—our worlds, our lives. Everyone together, the sky that we seldom see, the smile that is glanced at from time to time. And adoring love that is seen in the eyes of that beholder just to notice, to take notice of, to believe in love, and to enjoy your freedom and the very soul that lives inside and of an immortal promise that can be achieved.

—Steve Girten, December 2, 2011

The view of silence, with a vision of no sound, and in a realm of distant future, so profound, so unusual. But being limitless to the air and the sight of all things. The knowledge expands all around us. Like the wind with a subtle hint. Freedom can be offered through thoughts and the mind bright and focused. Sure as destiny, sure as love.

—Steve Girten, December 4, 2011

Am I ugly or beautiful? Is this my life, or can people see more? Seen on material value, and a way of past remembrance, to see, and then decide, who we really are.

—Steve Girten, December 3, 2011

"Stone of Life"

Stone of life that hangs to my chest, let me feel your power, the magical content showing way that you make things. The suggestion of feeling more, the being of safety. To be a believer of hope and not of fear. To see fear as a feeling of something to be beat. But in a spiritual life, the acceptance of things is a bit different. Although you stay proud and sure in your way of yourself and you're confident that your opinion is the best answer that you know. And that you're right because the true feelings of caring, helping, and loving. That keeps in order our actions, decisions, and what is right compared with what is wrong. A gift that is given to some—to trust a spirit of knowing of something that really isn't clear. And from the sky, a feeling of amazement, of an immaculate high.

In my life, I try to look for more—a spiritual way to live. For me, it's a way to care a little extra and that of passions. But not to tell people what you think is right or wrong but yet just give your opinion in average conversation. To finally encounter a spirit of something so holy, so to be adored, that it can't be wrong. Not just for all, considering the way that life can go and things that cannot be explained in reason. But there's always a way of hope, love. With a spirit, it's easier to overcome the fears in life. Life with so many meanings and to whom it applies to. What is heard, what is written, and what is seen. Just in the way a person communicates, his patience, understanding, gentle grace, care, a doctor, all authorities, the surgeon who has God in his hands.

Is love always true? That depends on the person involved. The sky so beautiful, and the clouds aren't always grey. Such as love and how life goes. With the sky above to notice, and the brotherhood of men to respect, just as we like respect to ourselves. And the street so dark and dirty, after the lust is gone, and of a murder in the near distance, when will people really see? Train of death, pass me by. Let me live in the future of the sky. Stone of life that hangs from my chest, maybe you can tell the rest.

—Steve Girten, March 27, 2009

Unfolding the magic, the beautiful sky, the horizon, the air we breathe. Our third planet—the third stone. Our three crosses, our one Jesus. The three pyramids. Disciples of the past, don't doubt us now, for we need your love. O, sun, with your burning light, keep us warm, keep us right! O, God, in our days of being lost, our belief grows. Our eyes begin to see, and then we know. The loss of confidence, the trust that's not trusted, and then the feeling of being forgotten and hurt. The pray that you acknowledge and understand, and we do. Signs of disaster, signs of death. The degrees of harm with an unbelievable loss to accept. Just hold out your hand and touch. Break through the fear and of any hurt that's so deep. Learn to give, learn to save, learn the old ways of life. The principles, the reasons for that we were taught. The meaning of life comes slow, and then at an older age, life matures and accepts wisdom. And to know life isn't over with. When you pass and leave, it's just a whole new way, with external love and peace, a feeling you don't want to miss.

—Steve Girten, February 28, 2010

The unconnected tribes of the third world. Their knowledge of any outside world is so limited. As of our countries, our cultures of wisdom, and our learning of history, technology beyond our own belief. The progression of knowledge, all the new electrical inventions, that has become common ways of life. But still, the tribe's primitive ways must be right. They seem to keep up with the living world. Maybe it's their strong belief that gives them so much power. Their spiritual worship and their brave and amazing pride.

—Steve Girten, January 17, 2017

The air that blows, the wheels that roll, the blocks that take their toll. The loss of people and friends and the gain of heartache and pain. And a subtle realization of nothing.

The head dying and the eyes crying, a lie trying. Is it just another day, or is it another night, hard to be certain, hard to be right? Was it because of you, or was it because of him? We smile, we lie, but is it a sin? I am lost looking in your eyes, the subtle feeling of loss, love for no reason—love that isn't wanted.

Beyond death and feeling of the bounds. Structures seeming to be an illusion as a new reality sets in. Curious is the sight that we see. A feeling of amazement is felt, almost penetrating through our skin.

—Steve Girten, 1990s

The simple fundamentals. The precious caring of life. But in a very different sight we see. We who have a mental disability or illness, we are often subjected to restrictions—that of housing, of freedom with society and money, and of healthy relationships. The outside life that was once so known now is just something that is so vague and forgotten. In the world out there, there is not much care, but the strong and brave know ways of power. And are beyond the hated world. But for us to get that far, we have to relearn ourselves to find inside the true, right respect to give as an adult in the progressive world. And to have true, honest pride in your life. Learn the work world. Be your own person. Have gratitude, have compassion, find love! To notice the way things are. To have patience, even when it's not easy. A feeling of hope and satisfaction, as well as giving it. Born at birth with a disability and doing no wrong and what kind of a chance.

The despair, sorrow of the life that has become so faded. Love as a hidden meaning. But to be able to pick yourself up and with no worries, confusion, or the pain. Yes to smile, to hear the birds sing. To feel the breeze and to enjoy your life. With the freedom of our society that is oh so free. And a change to find that new path to follow, a new dream, with anything that can be.

—Steve Girten, July 10, 2014

America, as clear as the summer skies above, we stand proud. With the freedom all around and with the trust of curiosity, we our strong. But the nonsettling feelings of attachment, greed, and power to control. But all this is just the basic ways of the human life. America's belief comes from the hearts of those who abide here. With the heart to care, the heart to share, and the knowing that this is to be used, to show love and to give love, giving the love that has been there and has been given to you.

—Steve Girten, January 4, 2017

Can the peace in our country beat the violence of theirs? The American way, so clear, so bright; love is in sight. With the night comes a feeling of bravery, pride, and of the summer's breeze with a hint of love. And with the sky that is so vast and endless over all the heads of us. Peace, love, freedom, pride, and belief. America!

—Steve Girten, April 10, 2013

And yes, humbled to Elvis. Let's not forget the king. Like a voice from heaven, he sings on. With his incredible, passionate moves. Bless the king who will never be forgotten—"Elvis Presley."

—Steve Girten, May 9, 2015

In presence, with the ability and how you are seen. There is always something that is seen by someone. Satisfaction—brave is the walk of life. Compassion is the open love, given by experience. Especially from those who are enlightened, wise, and patient with accepting everything that comes their way. Peace is a reward in life, a peace that should be shared. A life that has been very accomplished. Through thought and sacrifice and with the understanding of the world and of the people. But don't forget the greed of man. And that "love" is more than just a word.

—Steve Girten, August 6, 2014

Dimension of film/the actor's being of being a life that is not their own but to portray exactly their part. Just a role, just like life. To see a stranger but knowing that know a lot about you or something about you. But do they really know the truths of my life? Just an appearance with no secrets of worry. And the insight some ignore and or don't even give a chance of. The insight to notice—the clothes people wore, the shape of their body, messy or just dirty, clean, positive, outgoing, and of a smile. To hear their talk and with the connection with it. People's feelings—their plans, their losses, their accomplishments, and their laments. And if honest and a liar. People, just where have they been and where are they going to? The struggles in life, of a world at sight, how perfect can one be, and how perfect can one become! Was it death in some way that slows us down?

—Steve Girten, October 21, 2011

Our God, does He help a higher power or just help a lower, if not both? Shall the earth rise above after total devastation? And if it does, will a new world be prepared for us? And will it be similar to what humans remember in the world of the earth? The history of the earth can't be totally forgotten by life's existence. But of things in common interest, and will there be war, disease, famine, poverty? Will there be kings, queens, and ritual religion of anything ancient? Will there be any escape from the same old ways of life? And of a greed for self-want and a sin against man?

—Steve Girten, August 22, 2011

"Edgar Allen Poe"

Poe with all his energies, creation of imagination. As he focuses on the gust, he is with the wind. With a great collection of tales, his point prevails. With appreciation and gratitude of his amazing history. The drink wasn't enough but of the paper and pen. You live it, your life, and let it be, for so it will so remain forever.

—Steve Girten, January 23, 2007

It's not how but why. In your flow of passion, with no fear at all. Your love that will always protect your living in life. Be true, be you, and all the rest will follow.

—Steve Girten, January 23, 2017

The religion of music, with a sound of pure harmony— and an adoring sense. As in religion, there is a belief: all the fantastic energy that is shared. With patience of persistence and dedication, the determination of perfection, and the amazement of art that is completed. Music is intended for enjoyment, interest, and appreciation. And the respect of the talent. And actually, a feeling of love, or a great sadness, or just intrigue. Like religion, the meaning and message can be beyond doubt, truly incredible. A sense of mystery, a sense of excitement. Music can be similar to a spiritual encounter. Music can be worshipped by anyone at any given time and about anywhere. And is in the heads of many.

—Steve Girten, January 9, 2013

Where do the flowers go? Life goes on, but the tears remain. To listen to your song! On and on as we go, through the same meaning and the same patterns. But it's never enough of you. Have accepted you in any way that can be. Now that means without really ever to see your beauty again. But there is the vivid remembering of your voice, of your eyes, of your appearance, and of your life that I knew so well. The flowers of freedom will grow, and the ones that died, we grow again. And your song, my love, and the flowers were for you.

—Steve Girten, August 18, 2007

A soft kiss to your lips, perfume the scent so arousing. Come to me, in my twilight of witness, as we will be seen. Near I feel, feel you tight. Time begins to lose ideas. And with an immaculate act of our love and lives. An aura is felt and an adoring love that was only true feeling. Our soul may be at one, but I will follow your life through any shadow in the light, any darkness. And I would still know it's you.

—Steve Girten, July 6, 2007

Yesterday, not so far away, but to be enlightened of today. A brand-new way and day. Always on my mind. The heavenly feeling of words that aren't said but the meaning felt. My love, don't cry, for it's you I see and it's just me. The answer is to surrender, surrender your trust, and hope with the love we are thinking of.

—Steve Girten, June 13, 2007

To kiss your love, to see summer in your hair. I feel fine.

—Steve Girten, January 18, 2007

As I speak to "Mahumad," I begin to think of my first love. The words that people share and what is kept to be fair. Their sand our streets, with which for all our bare feet. To feel our air and a smile, the teeth give a warm security, safety in your vision.

—Steve Girten, January 24, 2007

"Do entities of the mind exist?"

I focus
I see you
I see all my surroundings
I have hope, and I know you are there.

Fragments of time—nothingness in ryhem. To touch the water and to see you crying. Religions of life, and of the thinking mind, we imply images of life. It forms until we are trusted, trusted as one.

—Steve Girten, January 24, 2007

"Predicting": a spiritual - attack. That will start page number 1, a Holocaust of its own rite. The United States may be realizing a spiritual movement of the third world. From a world of freedom we are so used to and very accepting of. But to think about our good country, a world doing good in many ways, and an exception of the violence and corruption, a greed for power. I mean our belief that I always will have faith with. Our belief that is proven in so many, many different ways, movements in each day. And it actually happens in a perfect fit at any time, and anywhere, and to the many, many different walks in life. What we need to notice is from place to place, ways are being known, known from not only the CIA or the FBI but of an spiritual power, at great distance or a very close one. The power of mouth that is changing, the precious communication that is not being made clear. Are all the precious past discoveries all gone? It seems never to be mentioned. And of what new history that is starting? Maybe the sky alone we will feel, with a great cry to let the earth feel the air blow, see the trees grow, watch the children learn, live for the love of faith. To be truly intrigued of knowledge, strength in your belief. And a tear to receive when you know there is no more you can do

—Steve Girten, Predicted on May 9, 2004; Written on January 20, 2017; Completed number 13 years later

The inspiration that I will bring, will last forever.

Wise as life lets me, let destiny take me.

A world killing, a world dying.

Ashes to ashes, dust to dust, the rest is up to us.

The meaning of life is the living of life.

They want me dead, but my soul won't allow them.

—Steve Girten, Date Unknown

O, Great Creator of our vast wonderful sky. Unfold your mystery upon me. Your sight is in my vision.

With every entrance I encounter brings a new direction in change. To hesitate as I do is for a reason of some control for an safe impression of all my surroundings and awareness.

—Steve Girten, Date Unknown

Signs of death: -
Signs of life: Myths destroy vulgar understandings of events
that exist.

Religion of gender. And to find your belief in existence. All so
many spirits. O, the many, many, many degrees and dimensions
and the endless worlds!

Paradox of life/passage to death.

—Steve Girten, Date Unknown

Refused in religion by universal remarks but with a way and
a prayer. Expressed belief goes far. Pleasant, the pleasant of
unearthly desire. Deserter of a cause. Ritual of wandered souls
casted out.

Dying inside, crying on the outside, just of the life to live. Smile
with the outside and keep the inside with perfect "Semitry of
Love."

—Steve Girten, Date Unknown

Hope with every spiritual encounter, the walk goes on.

There are many questions, but there are many answers too.

Mentally, physically, spiritually, that is the question.

Enhanced senses: sounds, colors, sight. Other is the confession
of the blind but how they feel.

—Steve Girten, Date Unknown

Appearance: dark, mysterious, and intrigued by fear. Is this going to be an encounter that will last forever? It's not even love but of the attraction felt.

—Steve Girten, January 22, 2017

I got music in me. I have my writings in me. I have the love to give to you, the given love that I was gave.

—Steve Girten, Date Unknown

Walking down the road, hearing what you are told. Do you know, oh, do you know? Your love is known and you are strong—with your beautiful smile. No tears are near; there will be no more tears but just the feeling of love . . . Your sweet, gentle touch of your "guster of compassion." Yes, your wonderful embrace, that of remembrance. And the trust in your voice. But to allow you to share my love, that's in my life. And to give acceptance to all the things that mean so much to me. But distant the feeling of love. Of opening my heart again and knowing to be mature with patience and trust. And with much experience and very familiar with the way, but it all seems new again. With age, the feelings are more understood. But keep your loving feeling that you have learned at a younger age. And remember the first teachings that you were taught and the way that it was shared.

—Steve Girten, October 3, 2013

Aware to aware, we sit and stare with hate and fear in our eyes. No cigarette to calm or hypnotize. And the pain and embarrassment that we feel. The medication or a fight. What time is it really? With just a bed the only comfort. What did we do, and where are we headed? And what can we do? Where are we suculsiond with no hope, no pride, and a loss of any respect and of a future that doesn't seem to matter? Breaking universal laws and maybe a sin of distant destiny. But does all this have a very special meaning, looking beyond the fear?

—Steve Girten, Date Unknown

The heavenly bird, soaring through the sky, so bright and so free. Imagine life so full of hope. Blue as the sky, our love is a love that's meant to be. Just seeing you in the summer's breeze, wanting a way for understanding. Missing time to talk with words so hard to come.

—Steve Girten, April 28, 2009

A practice for death, a wasted life some do say, but actually, it's a striving feeling of love, an adoring beauty of love of life. With always a love to complete. For a future that can't be beat.

—Steve Girten, February 19, 2010

I am fine now for a moment, was sad now for a moment. To say goodbye now but never to see you again. I am sad now for a moment, but I will carry through, at least for a moment. Bye, goodbye, to Shore Kare!

—Steve Girten, Day Program, September 30, 2009

Possessed by a love so adored, Jim, are you still there?

—Steve Girten, January 24, 2007

When we pass away, all your world shall follow. With the destiny of life, with accomplishments and pride. Just you remember to truly accept the love that is given. And don't frown upon the negative, yet celebrate who you are! Everyone has to live, and everyone has to die. Think of the present and hope for the future, "and live not for yesterday." Be brave and accept!

—Steve Girten, March 4, 2009

In the world, there are vacant spaces that we all come across from time to time. Does this interest you? Or do you just turn and ignore of any meaning with this happening? Does hearing something at first notice? Throw off your judgment of what is really meant. The words of meaning. Do things that aren't clear make you wonder? Do you try to look beyond this, the things that don't seem clear?

—Steve Girten, September 7, 2015

*

Gone like the summer's breeze of night!

The inspiration that I bring will last.

Wise as life lets me, let destiny take me.

—Steve Girten, 2015

Colored haze flows with filtered air as she sits meditating, drifting through her mind. I wait, watching, asking without a word but wanting an answer. As the cool breeze comes and awakes our attention. Suddenly, we feel a sense of relief. Now we resume back into our own dreams and life.

—Steve Girten, Date Unknown

Looking into your eyes of mystery. So subtle and deep you appear. Are you as you look? So vague! A feeling that you give but of interest and of lust. The wonder of touch, to feel your body and all the love that you may give. To share a life with physical acceptance. To honestly accept the true feelings before any lust that might become. "Love may be found!"

—Steve Girten, October 4, 2015

It's not only what the young can do for the old but what the old can do for the young as well.

—Steve Girten, September 9, 2015

The memories of old dreams, awake at the most precious moments, of satisfaction, achievements, and gratitude. There is a love that's never going to be forgotten.

—Steve Girten, November 13, 2015

The timing of an era. From time to time, the world changes. I have understood it, and I have learned from it. For many decades of studying a knowledge of acceptance. And being ready for enlightenment. But the new world after mine. After my power and meaning and of my name. But although the old world will still exist but in a different way. The newer power learns from the past powers, but fresh in its timing. After all, love is love and of all and all.

—Steve Girten, March 29, 2009

To visit, and a carpet on the floor and a happy bottle near a door. I am once again here. The love is always the same shared. To be with you is an adored feeling of contentousness. And while we talk, we dream together. Our deep understandings of words and of a clear memory of voice. As the evening comes and the night finally arrives, to realize what might be so considered. The body and the mood—feeling close and soon. Like a new birth, that struggles with suggestions of growth, like the meaning of the air! "That's all around us." Comparing fragile to wonder.

—Steve Girten, Date Unknown

The animals of this earth, roaming both old and young, in captivity or in the wild. Especially for the young children who have a bond with all the beautiful animals. The love in their eyes, of a beauty of an adored sight, of such creatures! The excitement for the kids and all the great memories to remember—for the whole family. Animals are important to the times, just like us humans who have their place in our world.

—Steve Girten, Date Unknown

The warmth that saved my soul, the dying winter, and the strive for life. And for the ability to keep the things that are important. The pain now almost gone, for the sun has come and all is done. As another night comes, and another month, and another day. And when it's all done and when it's all said, our love will still remain true.

—Steve Girten, Date Unknown

In the days of Jesus, when people wandered and walked amazed, and the sight of the sky was adored, there was more than just the three crosses, more than just his teachings; there was a feeling of trust, a knowing to follow. Helping a belief that soon would be worshipped forever. The strength of Jesus, His will, and His unconditional love for all. The cross is the will of life for life. And the church helps us remember.

—Steve Girten, April 21, 2010

"Have You Noticed?"

In the dark, there is still a light, either outside or inside. Without the sun, without any lamp. There is a vision of hope and love. Remember to see, look beyond the obvious. There will be a way. "Just notice."

—Steve Girten, April 11, 2010

Now bound to living back in the community, wow, how the years have gone. The outside is so near and so different the fear.

—Steve Girten, Date Unknown

"America Like Heaven/
In God We Trust"

Paused for a day and accepting in a new way. Inspire the way of knowledge. Strong and sure, bright and right. The dreams that hold us together. Received by a pray or something in the air with pushing the bounds of spiritual realms. Is the soul much different from our heart, is our life much different from one another? Are all religions with the same destiny? The precious undetermined ways of acts enjoy the intended silence of surety.

—Steve Girten, February 26, 2007

Beyond the wisdom of an era and left alone in a world, a world of confusion. At this time and moment, the earth shall raise, and all the seas will become one, and our land will become water. But the sky itself will remain unchanged. In this deleted state, beings won't be found, and a search for brotherhood is needed. But the galaxies of all the universe will shift, and time is forgotten. Will deep vision of all everlasting promise of true reality sustain the test?

—Steve Girten, May 30, 2012

The special children, just look in their eyes and see their sadness inside. Lonesome are they—the forgotten lives. The alone feeling that basically keeps them alive. The suffering alone feeling that shouldn't be there. And that feeling that holds them back with restrictions and to not able to accomplish anything meaningful. But their purpose does have significance and of great meaning. For the vacant eyes that don't see so well, they really love the feeling of compassion.

—Steve Girten, December 28, 2011

"Dead, Are We?"

The remaining from mishaps in recurrences of life. And with the natural balance of the way things work, we were passed by—like forgotten. But to realize this to have a purpose and/or meaning. For we are gifted and special. To care as we do and to help as we see it. And some with the ability to understand love and give that love as they feel it. The tears that fall from the cruel world, and the disgrace with a tragic, suffering time is happening. The sad, lonely feeling, just from a love we feel that should be given and shared. Mental illness is a disorder, and life is life, diseased or not.

—Steve Girten, Date Unknown

The beauty that people see remains in me.

The state lies, and the church tells the truth.

Trust, love, compassion, ability of enlightenment.

The pain and sins of this world, shall I just lay myself
down in torment within a heaven of forever peace?

—Steve Girten, April 19, 2012

The human existence/final awakening is our universe.

—Steve Girten, August 2, 2012

The beauty that they see with love in their eyes. The forgotten
they are but still in memory, they remain. Although they strive
through their journey in life, sad is the basic feeling. Lost but
still concerned. With bravery and a will of compassion, that will
prove love and for it to be always remembered.

—Steve Girten, March 21, 2012

A kiss of a lifetime, like a star, we see fall from the sky. Your life won't be forgotten. The way you shone and what you gave. Your love that changed a generation or two. Just your appearance, perfect as you. And a determined mind that cannot be stopped. A burning flame of lust, power, and greed—"all for love." But then life becomes too slow for your pace, but in a younger age, that wouldn't matter. But that didn't stop you, and nothing ever will. Heaven will be your next adventure, and it is ready for you! And God bless you for what's to come!

—Steve Girten, December 25, 2011

To not love and never have tried doesn't mean your right in the long run. But to always try to find love and wonder why it's so hard to achieve and feel. And when you are about to give up and have had it for the last time, love is found. A surprised feeling that suddenly came. To share love is one of the most precious gifts.

—Steve Girten, December 29, 2011

"Mom/Shirley"

Mama, Mama, Mom, how much I love you. The way you kept me safe when I was young and letting me find my own life in times of learning. And for your trust in me, for when honesty and respect was proven. I live with my love, the love I give, and especially from the love you gave.

—Steve Girten, November 20, 2012

Love

Belonging to the world, with nonunion. In a separate reality, not from anything known. Almost in degrees of surreal dimensions together lost in a spiral void and floating unbound in the wind, up in the sky not seen. Here is where there is no words, just feeling.

—Steve Girten, May 30, 2012

No hostility, just adoring in its entirety. Here, we are free; here, we are safe. We are confident, and we are sure. A bright, clear environment of all surroundings. Golden are the eyes that see.

—Steve Girten, May 30, 2012

"As We Reflect"

As of our vision, the world unfolds. With around us, we imitate of what the fear is, the hope, the hate, and the love. Like seeing the societies as individuals and watching the flow of everyday struggles in life.

—Steve Girten, September 12, 2012

World of device: The electronic world is taking over. And nature, as we know it, does suffer with the beauty of such freedom, and even the peace that it brings is being and becoming ignored and then forgotten and faded out.

—Steve Girten, September 12, 2012

The more we experience in life, the greater our world can be. But of the good and bad that will occur.

—Steve Girten, August 19, 2012

Is sex a sin? Or just a pleasure that shouldn't be? But making love is a feeling that everyone should experience.

—Steve Girten, August 9, 2012

The youth of a new generation that may follow my history in this world. Although in a different age in time but yet will still live and share at the same meaning of time.

—Steve Girten, August 19, 2012

"Never Ending"

A peace given from shared existence. As like the air and breath we take. As of the sight of perception—the beauty all around. The love that comes from the souls that give. Treasure the moments of the feeling of love. Create your spiritual being in life.

There are many worlds, but there's at least one that should be believed in.

—Steve Girten, August 9, 2012

To the silent rockers, *believe and achieve*!

—Steve Girten, March 21, 2012

The mind, my mind, *my mind.* Drifting, flowing through the dark forces and of unknown realms. Just the common fresh scent of the breeze. I reflect on as the air around becomes known.

—Steve Girten, August 2, 2012

In your dark eyes, I see a vision of contentment. The lost look, but you're very focused, deep and pleasing, mysterious, and misleading. The love you prove and the love that you make. But given with patience and grace, cool as the breeze. "I see you at ease." Your appearance like an image of intrigue, interest, amazement. So sad and intense you're going, but forever I will know.

—Steve Girten, September 27, 2012

Forgiveness of beginning and ending.

—Steve Girten, October 4, 2012

The experience of death and of the leaving of life.

—Steve Girten, October 7, 2012

Your name to be heard and your voice to be remembered. Your name not said, but your love that is felt inside by many. Your image—the way you are, who you are, and what you do. Are you proud? Have you accomplished a passion or a dream? Do you have a clear outlook in life? Is there cheer in your life and/ or happiness? Do you have a direction, a purpose to find, plans of accomplishments? Has true love found you, and do you still search for love?

—Steve Girten, Date Unknown

I have walked the earth in a theory of life. And in my unconsciousness. Stars and colors all surrounding. Images are familiar but vague and not related. In a vision of lost ambition. A struggle to attach is needed, a clinging to be found. I've walked the earth, I've seen the sun, and I've noticed that young that run and have fun. And I have seen the tears, and I have felt the fears.

—Steve Girten, September 22, 2012

Often, I wonder of the many ways of life, of existence, of my ability, and of the human appearance of our structure in being. Everything fits so nicely but to have a safe destination—with karma, belief, and love. And a prayer that can possibly help. We're all different; we're all the same. Enjoy this crazy world of love.

—Steve Girten, 2012

Life is so creative but such a remorse way it feels. To give and want love—how terrifying the idea. The applauds of a society, watching curiously and wanting a satisfaction that will please. But the lonely souls that try and never seem to find the luck. But they too have a purpose of progression on this earth. Never a waste to the human appearance, for they are already dead.

—Steve Girten, October 1, 2015

The searching of knowing that there might just be a great purpose and or meaning to this world of knowledge.

—Steve Girten, September 28, 2015

The love of family that can be as strong as religion. But with the lament of family, it can be as deep as death. But the love of life, to live, and of many decisions made. The happiness, the sorrow, and the gain and the loss and with a very strong passion—life will grow. To find compassion at a time, you will know to keep it. And embrace it through the rest of your life. I'm determined with love—to spread it, to share it.

—Steve Girten, August 3, 2015

"Season"

The naked trees and the cold breeze. What is this season coming to be? Is this our last winter? Or the last of its kind? Feeling a change but very unsure, a vague fear is felt. With a changed world. From Russia to America, through Europe and the islands, and Egypt too. The sky with its dark intent. Does the sun exist? Is there a single star in the sky? Are we the creatures of the earth meager forms of subjective views?

—Steve Girten, October 15, 2012

"The Wonder"

From electricity to the telephone, to the climate weather that is now being predicted ahead of time. The precious medical advancements that have saved so many lives. Traveling—cars, busses, trains, planes, and ships that are so monitored, the sky, the sea. The people of the earth are in control. The satellites for knowledge and for protection now a creative electronic fascination that passes time and pacifies the active mind. As this world has been growing, just what if our very universe has been growing just as much.

—Steve Girten, September 28, 2015

"Young Earth"

In the beginning, the world so cold, empty, and vacant - destillent. But with an immaculate force of power from the sky, the earth was born. Nature became adored. And so much water. But before Christ, the ancient world of cultures that took over and very original. Today there is still a very interesting sight and history, of their beliefs and of their ways. And the remains are all still as mysterious and enlightening. But nowadays in the states, everyone seems to have a greed for want, for whatever attracts them. The rushed societies that struggle to make it. With so many types of people who our trying to live their own lives. But the ones who walk with so much pain in their eyes and those who make plans to accomplish. And a love that is found and a love that has been looked for. But even with love, there is pain. So enjoy life but be ready for whatever may come.

— Steve Girten, September 28, 2015

"Emotional"

Feeling on a basic level. To keep in touch with your feelings, to control a certain sense of your way. Maybe to be more passive and less aggressive, or more aggressive and less passive. And put bye, the worries of your day, with a night that prepares for your new tomorrow.

—Steve Girten, August 24, 2007

To remember freedom from a young age. To remember when you read a book at school and knowing it was cool and to really hug your mother after you have cried. And to show appreciation to your father when he comes home from work. To realize life is hard but with gratitude to have in the way that you live your life. Believe, there will never be another one like you.

—Steve Girten, August 24, 2007

The tall frosted trees of November, the beauty of God is in sight. The cold winter's chill pureitizing my air to the open night. For miles a silent walk, of this heavenly night. Not a soul around, trying to seek meaning. The cold becoming too much—home is in need. A tear comes down my cheek from my left eye. Not a tear of sorrow but a tear brought from this cold night.

—Steve Girten, November 2015

Surrealizium/the occult—dark mystery and intrigue: the sun. The moon and myths of the old. Possession of our own soul. Our mind and body, the feeling of our emotions, both pain and beauty. A tear and a smile, it's all the same. But this is a part of life, to know it or not. What is that scared sense you have? Is it a fear of change of the unknown? And what of your ability to understand it?

—Steve Girten, December 1, 2015

What is love, and what is hate? Is it nothing but emotions that we feel? The very soul itself is filled of love, with an energy of power such like our universe. Oh, the wonder, oh, so precious as the being we are on earth. Delicate as a butterfly, seen at a glance. The white dove soaring through the skies, displaying love, spreading peace and beauty.

—Steve Girten, October 5, 2015

The love I have is not just of you and also not just for the close family. But a love of peace for humanity in the world. And of similar ways in life that we all share. And for the compassion of a nation that begins a trust, with trust. And the holiness that is still felt, given by the old and those who pray. And an awareness of those who seek. My love is for you.

—Steve Girten, March 27, 2012

Have you witnessed the beautiful expression of nature? At plain sight of the trees, the birds, and the grass that grows, with the flowers that show. Just the feeling of the enlightened forest. To stumble into the peace and/or harmony. To relieve yourself of all morbid and hatred ways of being.

—Steve Girten, January 13, 2016

"Silence/Love of Wisdom"

The next world and spiritual realms, a symbol or image

The tarot and astrology and the self-realization of a dimension opened and offered upon us to find another world. A shared journey to higher ways. Like a temple with hope and filled mystery. Focusing on breath, our awareness is enlightened, enhanced, and crystallized.

—Steve Girten, October 2, 2015

"Inspire—a Perception"

The modesty of a culture with pride and with strong beliefs in their way. But so many paths of structured life and religion that covers so many answers. The flow of the twenty-first century—a total external world. All the wants but little notice of the precious things. Is our destination headed to a good or a bad outcome, and for any distant life, will it be about the same will as we know?

—Steve Girten, December 15, 2011

With a guide, I ride high, with a tear, I miss you because of the fear that's coming so near. The rainbows and the stars, the wind and the pain—different and now the same. Under and of the above peace, love for everyone. Follow now, just not in sorrow. A belief of precious love forever, and I see it in your eyes. I keep a picture of your eyes in my mind of memory. And the charm that came. Beautiful ocean of dreams—the days come, and the days go. The young child playing in the sand. As there is time and there is no time. Your smile alone brightens my night. And just to reflect of all that has gone.

—Steve Girten, 2007

Meditation, circle shapes, and chants. The gradual loss of perception, with a reality to dream while being awake. To create to know your thoughts and feelings, with meaning.

Friends talk, strangers walk, the stars shine and rhyme. The need of greed, the soft birth, and the tragic death. But not beyond yet, an apocalyptic feeling of life. That just came as the morning of day, that of your appearance that will never be seen again.

—Steve Girten, 2007

A man sweating. But of now, the water beads off his body.

Compelling our bodies in hope of creating a new life. Just us and with no external interference, just for us to complete this plan. A child of love.

The fresh smell of season, so free without reason. To adore, 'cause maybe no more.

—Steve Girten, 2007

Beneath the sea, above the sky, my love cries to see your face to have forsaken beyond the torment and ache.

Now playing death game's with the old for a way to live. For life is uncertain. With talk, the laughs, and the tears and oh, the young feelings. Distant hope of destiny and the seeing of a stranger. The disadvantage of money and the loss of love.

—Steve Girten, Date Unknown

I have seen you today. It wasn't the same as yesterday. Today I love you, and tomorrow I am sad. Your love hurts me so bad. To see you and then wanting to feel you. To be with you and then without you.

Where do people go? What do I care? *Will they grow?* Leaving and yelling, gone and mad. So telling alone now and sad.

—Steve Girten, 2007

Candle light and safe music fitting the mood, the ambiance of perfection. With a girl and a bottle, words and a poem. A kiss that lasts and another that seemed to pass. To brighten a day but to miss you whenever you go away.

The brain, thinking, seeking, retaining, striving for the best of ability. PERFECTION!

—Steve Girten, 2007

Having a name and emotions, wanting credit for efforts completed and of own self-esteem. Embracing, gripping for life with no love and no hate. The loss of you, I do learn from, to bury the past and justify the present. And not to deprive love in your condition of life. To describe without using a knife and of a gun in hand. And to just notice the eyes that care; there is always someone who's gonna be there!

—Steve Girten, 2007

Today is the way I feel, and no one can take it away. It is mine, and it is real. I feel your love 'cause love is what is felt.

The child crying of love, looking for someone, something to stop the pain.

—Steve Girten, 2007

Strengths and weaknesses. Remember the good, what you could, and not the bad and to be sad. A smile, a handshake, to yell and/or to hate. To awake and open your eyes, to feel the day, to notice the ground decay, and to just walk away and let this day pass nicely away.

—Steve Girten, 2007

Fundamentals, that which is lived, and to have the gain of control to feel self-worth. Is the space between each of us, individual to another? Is it possible that this space is filled with a power of love? An aura of intention to be known. To find love, which is to be never expected, it must first come from the internal. As our hearts learn from the struggles of happiness, sadness, grief, abandonment, sorrow, torment, true love, and the feeling of being so alone. But life will be rewarded—as in proper the effort.

—Steve Girten, January 13, 2013

Enter Egypt; exit your world. The sand we walk, so soft and dry. Even the sky appears different, an almost seen meaning, and of the amazement, that of the pyramids. The inner beauty of Egypt lies within the Great Pyramids of Giza. The adoration of the colored painted history of their past beliefs and societies. A story of visitors from above and of a belief that became worshipped. The drawings and symbols with their special meanings, those were meant to last.

—Steve Girten, April 3, 2014

"Intention"

To free my expressions of feelings. To open my heart and mind and to accept the true feelings of knowledge I acquire.

—Steve Girten, December 6, 2012

Does love shine as bright as the sun?

—Steve Girten, January 14, 2013

With music, there is no attachment, just free is the feeling.

—Steve Girten, February 2, 2012

Within philosophy, I find I am not alone. With music it is shared, a cool feeling of excitement and of appreciation. An overwhelming sense of happiness. Like the conversations between two in love. And of an emotion to touch, feel that is intimate. At best, music can be adored. And the caress of which is felt becomes an encounter of much more expected or even guessed.

—Steve Girten, December 23, 2012

Reflection in my mind, answering to degrees in time, of the memory stained and bruised. "Now I stand accused." The fright of being made wrong, and the fear if it's true, and then the torment of that loss. In future ways, we have a hint of hope that things will be better, but actually, that's not promised; you never know quite what to expect. When you get older and used to being mature, a bonus aspect is your life is filled spiritually, and if following of a higher power, your wisdom will exceed. And when that hint of hope comes, the older the better to let things come as they occur.

—Steve Girten, March 15, 2011

I am content; I am creative. I see my focus, and I will follow my dreams. I believe in a great compassion of brotherhood, a striving of love to give, from with the love I was given. An inner peace of accomplishment and self-fulfillment. I love the things I see, I love the things I feel, but just for how long will I carry this love—the love I have, the love I am able to give?

—Steve Girten, October 4, 2012

Ideas that conjure within the mind and the decisions that we make, that assure. But to be bold, strong, and confident, knowing right from wrong, *being mature*. Remembering love even when there seems to be none.

—Steve Girten, January 13, 2013

As the rain comes, your head in the sky, as I see you, and as you drift on bye. And I know the love I see in your eyes. And as I touch you, stranger to stranger, into our lives. Will I fall in love with you, and will the people have compassion and let our love flow?

—Steve Girten, October 3, 2012

Let your children learn. Give them the time that they need. Show them interest and that you care. But although it's not so easy to express the feelings of concern. To love as if it's your own life and also to give exceptions in ways of worries and of faith. To try to put out your time and patience, but it seems never to be appreciated and even disregarded. The love of father, the love of mother; and the love of the child.

—Steve Girten, February 3, 2012

Way of compassion. And time for reality. Knowing the flow of life and, in general, societies at pace. And our attention should be focused on the control of intellectual power, the feelings with gain, that should be proper. Oh, but all the greed and self-want. But pity will find them. So keep your head up high and keep our land clean, bright, clear and right.

—Steve Girten, February 2, 2012

"Is It All the Same?"

So much of changes in the general public, ways of life. Life reproducing life. And the nations of the past and future, but what about the present that seems to be forgotten or ignored? Religions through the ages, what's remembered and accepted. Faces and names and many stories. Thoughts combined to form a belief. Through the unknown, it will be remembered with power and of meaning. All in all, is it? Or is it the very way of karma of the things that we do.

—Steve Girten, February 7, 2012

Whatever my image is and the appearance that is seen by the human life of others. But my reflection shown and whatever decisions that are made. Does your love show, or is it kept so deep inside, or do you think you always show your love?

—Steve Girten, November 19, 2013

Adventure is what you want, to know the weather by the way the wind blows or to kill when handed a knife. "With an intent of evil. Or is it too hard for you to smile or to share some kind of love? It is waiting for you whenever you're ready?"

—Steve Girten, August 21, 2014

How to acquire was of life such as the love that I have for you?
To know how you feel and to see what's real.

—Steve Girten, April 7, 2014

I live my life like the United States runs our country. We are
brave, we are strong, we help one another. We help protect other
countries in need and assist whatever is really in need because
that's the way we are. To be an American, you must believe.

—Steve Girten, April 8, 2014

Breaking through and with strange days. Leads us to the soft
parade for an LA woman. Light my fire—an American poet.
Waiting for the sun at his hotel. The end.

—Steve Girten, August 15, 2015

A face, the eyes/wisdom from a dream, distant stone shapes, the ancient and said. The nights with their full moon/creative and wandering the dark mysteriously pondering. Your body, my life, your life, our bodies. Our feeling in one. Our souls that have won.

—Steve Girten, August 15, 2015

In a lifetime of an era, I am with the world, now with the trees and of the breeze, the birds' gentle grace that flies through the air. To see the dark and care as if it were light. And your eyes, the eyes I don't see anymore, so lost in a vague distraction of feelings that pain I see in your smile, of anyone's eyes, and a tear that comes that makes me forget, and a sad left impression of abandonment—*so alone*. The sheets that I hide under wanting no more and the sight of people that makes me remember. But the love that I can't give up, it will always remain.

—Steve Girten, September 22, 2011

Coda of my life from the simple explanations of life to the deep, deep meanings of death, truth, realms of belief, and my life. I struggle for a life that I don't have and what I really am looking for, for some kind of an enlightenment of a future. As I grow and go through ways of earthly conformity, I notice that love has a way to find itself just at the night times. When things are unexpected and when there is a cool feeling. But through worldly beliefs and possessions and the relationships of understandings, life is basically how you feel. Let me white as because it does help me feel.

—Steve Girten, September 28, 2013

Oh, Vicki girl! Oh, Vicki girl! You're so shy look but so full of curiosity, intrigue that really attracted me. Our playing of feelings that became love, a very serious love—one of companionship, one of sex. And one of loss, loss of being together. No more to see and out of time. Sad is the memory with all the excitement of a first love from within. And Vicki's face still I reflect.

—Steve Girten, June 20, 2013

Vicki, I gave a baby too, from her and me. That was to show our love. But I was never able to be a father. A father who shows love to his child.

—Steve Girten, April 7, 2014

Birthdays/deaths—life's ways! The hidden meaning of our being in life. The cheer and the fear, oh, what's so near! The air, the sky, and a sad kiss goodbye. In your eyes, I can see a hint of confusion, of being lost. Maybe it's the pain that has bruised your very soul.

—Steve Girten, June 2013

The unspoken, unspoken words that are never heard. All the love that is hid inside.

—Steve Girten, April 7, 2014

As I see, as I see the break of the sun, the sky opens and the signs of fun has begun. To wake, not wanting to fake, but just to make, make a difference—something positive. The day's ahead, and the night that is now gone. Run, run with the wind. See endless to the sky. For you are free with a heavenly notice that shall keep you safe. Be proud, be free, sail on. There's a light that follows all your dreams, all your love. Not needing anything but just to see.

—Steve Girten, June 2013

Fears, the belief of something we should face. Environment, to control that is of power—empowerment. The greed and lust of some just to force their point. And but the love of all things—as peaceful, no fears, and every surrounding "that of beauty and that of passion.

—Steve Girten, February 13, 2013

The children's ways of life, in the year of 2013, are still not yet determined.

—Steve Girten, May 4, 2013

The abandonment of life, with no attachment, and free the flow of love. The beautiful aura of the being that is. At this point, you may be pure, pure of desire, lust, greed, and the hatred of all societies. The invited human physical appearance. And a death that wants payback. The aura, the freedom, the purity of this do not last, and then that of your appearance will be no more. And the soul itself shall remain—in meaning.

—Steve Girten, May 4, 2013

A meaningful life: A meaning life begins with truth and honesty. And then to have pride and confidence, this is a good way to learn compassion. With the respect that you give, a feeling of accomplishment and gratitude will be found. As with age, the recurrences we go through as we learn and understand, and when we grow, wisdom is acquired. And as we share and as we love, life can become a wonderful and spiritual place.

—Steve Girten, January 15, 2013

We can't control our pain and not exact with the future that we yet not know of. But we can through accepting of things that we can't change and to keep compassion in our hearts. To truly be open-minded and not judgmental of people, all the nations, race, creed, ethnic, belief, color of skin, and daily problems. So keep your hope, and share it wherever you go. And remember; patience with a smile and to find your own destiny.

—Steve Girten, January 15, 2013

The freedom found at a young age, later to become wisdom at an older age.

—Steve Girten, June 5, 2013

Trying to find a passage for either my destiny or a new world. For with my hope in this world seems like it's no longer to be found. But a strong love I shall always have within my being, within my soul.

—Steve Girten, June 10, 2013

After I become truly complete, I will be full circle.

—Steve Girten, May 28, 2013

To those whose talents are unnoticed, all the beauty that they have done, but with a gift that hides, sleeping and just is in their own world, waiting to be found by the public, societies, even nations, the world of all people of any creed on race, the sky is the limit—or is it?

—Steve Girten, May 28, 2013

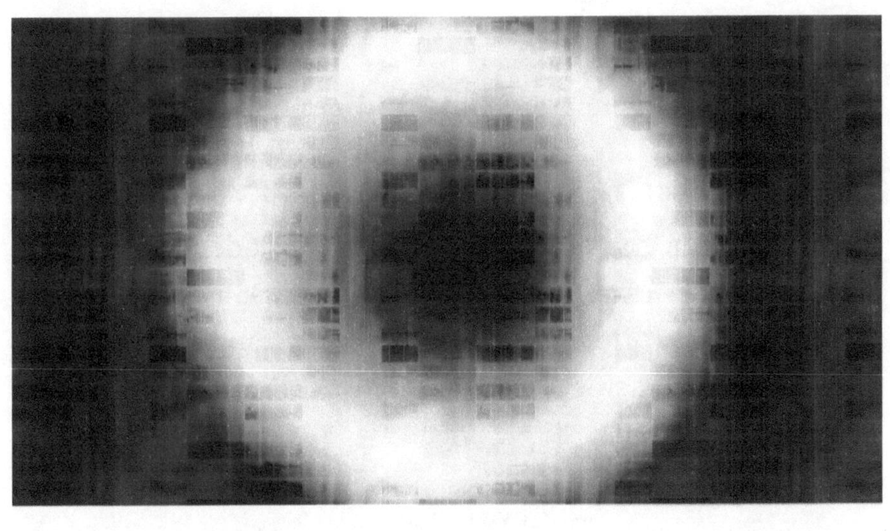

Banned from a world I love, to ascend to a new world I don't know of yet.

—Steve Girten, May 27, 2013

With nature, it seems to be the only love in this evil world.

—Steve Girten, May 27, 2013

The past shows for itself whoever can plan it.

—Steve Girten, May 27, 2013

Lord, I am with you from time to time. Now understanding with a given trust and proud of your attention. I think of you as I think of myself. In this world, a belief is needed for whatever your way is. In the quiet of the night, a sudden sense is felt. Could this be fear from a loss of spirit or of being? To the people, to the world, the feelings of trust, caught, delight. As we breathe as to achieve, we might just realize how wonderful life is.

—Steve Girten, 2013

To see the tears from hatred and the fears that brought it. The ignorance of man that fits with all things in life. Hate, love, sadness, happiness, and gain and loss. The freedom that some find and of the torment that is never really planned. A love that can go a long ways but only seems to end in sorrow.

—Steve Girten, Date Unknown

The more we learn and accomplish, the greater the cause for good and bad to occur.

—Steve Girten, May 22, 2013

Hey, do you know, I know the things of distance, dark and clear? I see the unknown, and my timing in life is so exact that my appearance is slightly slower. But of the pride that we should always have, to be proud of what we do and satisfied with thoughts or decisions that we make. To always be strong with our belief and open-minded to questions that come. You shouldn't criticize what you don't understand.

—Steve Girten, May 22, 2013

The Sensitivity of Societies

The blame of guilt they put on the suffering ones. The lust that preys of the young and innocent. But the elders who save and practice, respect and patience, in stride they go. And through the love of brotherhood, the night hints of togetherness. The dark with intrigue brings surprise and enjoyment for those ready. To share love is the most joyful feeling. And it will come, and you will experience it. Time has a funny way for things to be.

—Steve Girten, December 29, 2011

Behind you, with all the love in the world. As I watch you, it is with pride and admiration. Safe you are, and safe you will stay. Because your love will save nations.

—Steve Girten, December 5, 2011

A Mother's Love from God

As giving life. A mother's intuition of love is given. As of God. Her sacred love must be given. The baby, so innocent like a flower in the breeze, so vulnerable of disease, sickness, pain. With the brain new, unbalanced, there is a constant challenge to keep thinking and to retain.

> —Steve Girten, April 26, 2012

Am I here, there, or anywhere? With the figuring of life and of time will define the right rhyme? Will I, you, find the happiness that life offers, the way of life that struggles to find the truths that we are all looking for? And to beat all the hatred, the greed, the violence, and the temptations that throw off our judgments and direction of the flow of life and of love.

> —Steve Girten, May 22, 2013

Are you experienced? Jimi was. Through his purple haze, he had a vision, and he made incredible sense out of it. And his extraordinary talent with his guitar. It was more than music, and so was he—Jimi Hendrix.

> —Steve Girten, Date Unknown

Angels that we are, with a bit difference in ways of common life. Our special condition of having died in so many ways. And of our feelings, so sensitive and with a love that which we long for but also to give as much of that love back, and every bit of compassion and warmth is assertive so. Unconditional ways of caring but so low of our feelings that we get. Hurt and even some pain, our suffering of our "mental illness," which usually happens from birth. How can such a natural way of living be wrong, that of the human brain? The brain like the weather, of natural events, the sky, the sun, and of all growing things, and our universe, and of the unknown. The brain, all our brains, relates to all things and is eager for new intrigue and mystery of enlightenment. *Enjoy your journey.*

—Steve Girten, February 8, 2013

A chill from above. Having had heaven for quite a long time but lately now in a different sense—*this chill*. Does this feeling come with a meaning in a new unknown way of hope and change? But so much the fear of destiny that is certain to come. All leading to a final destination, end of this life.

—Steve Girten, February 1, 2012

As the evening comes, and the sun has gone down, and the warm breeze of summer that flows through our hair. The sight of love is felt all around. The feeling of hope, trust, compassion that is shared. On this evening, one should meet another and become one. And a movement of faith that is felt and kept inside and even to the others around.

—Steve Girten, February 1, 2012

The circles in the universe, sun, and God and the universal love that is there. Morning, evening—the snake represents the realm of mystery. To follow in path—"nature and the sky." The power of darkness/shadows that we notice.

Deities' sayings are now letters and words from the stars. When you look for a feeling of magic and immaculate of intrigue in the air. You may notice the clouds are fair and the mood of heaven has come, and when the sky is dark and lightning strikes, and a ball of fire sets a new day, deliberate prayers depart and soon fade away.

—Steve Girten, Date Unknown

God, meditation, and music. The beauty and harmony of belief. The extra sense of security, safety, and even peace. Do you realize that love is all around? And do you remember the fun and trust of the innocents that was there as a child, just learning "We are accepting the things that interest us," and common knowledge of young ways? The beautiful child's head, so fragile, without limits.

—Steve Girten, June 18, 2012

The invisible air is gold for us to share.

You

One thing I love is to kiss a pretty girl's face, one thing I love is peace to the human race, one thing I love is to be free, to do what I want, to be clean, to be happy, to be satisfied, to have money, and to be with you.

—Steve Girten, Date Unknown

Actions with every move, violence that leads to death. Thoughts that linger and peace, peace has to be accomplished. Of the shrine of life and a celebration of realization, of happiness.

Flowers in your hair just to feel the air. Up and down like a kid kneeling on the floor, running, laughing, seeing all around, the love just to be found.

—Steve Girten, Date Unknown

The willpower to beat eventuality, with a pause and wish, the pain would go. Similar situation that is gone. But a second reason for it to stay. With the world that belongs to everyone, do your part or leave.

Sacred girl, the sun is up, and the drink is poured. Your hug is near, but you are not here.

—Steve Girten, Date Unknown

To see the sight of day, looking, turning, knowing to pray.

Licensed to trust—life is loaned out. To travel—sand and water, the drugs, music, sex, or rape. Resorting to a memory as a way of life. Feeling desperate and dirty.

—Steve Girten, Date Unknown

Image's shadow, the sun. Fingers feeling the sand. From you a wet kiss on my check, clothes covering the body. Naked to the universe, with rhymes and aspects forgotten. Waves—emotions, light, sounds. Slow I feel, perceiving my appearing.

Wet feeling—compilation brightened. Releasing of lust and then love. And the lonesome cult long-lived.

—Steve Girten, Date Unknown

Unique the mind discovering. Other subconsciousness, unconsiousness—galaxies of an unlimited universe. Like animals that demonstrate their past age. In decades, humans related. Dimensions in time and space. Crystal life appears. Bright the vision but distorted, sensitivity with a complex nature, running, hiding, knowing of change. Concept appeared aspects.

—Steve Girten, Date Unknown

Suggestive muse, invading members with faith and past divinity of holiness in knowledge. Beautiful!

Seeing darkness, deep darkness. Seeing the world closing in, finding people disappearing. Through and through, the night goes on, and the nights will win. Solutions, confusions—the light that shines in through the darkness. A moon that glows in the sky. A little cute girl who cries after a night so divined.

—Steve Girten, Date Unknown

Tribes of peace—priest in ceremony, temple like the universe. To wonder with the knowledge. Mystical quests and dreams— spiritual enlightenment.

Summary of suffering and pain. Ceremony unfolds life in cycles, rebirth, religious belief. Life and death contrast manifests in a new innate feeling like a child of ideas. Life immaculate as of all our beings.

—Steve Girten, Date Unknown

Aware to aware, we sit and stare with hate and fear in our eyes, no cigarette to calm or hypnotize. And the pain and embarrassment we feel. The medication or the fight, what time is it really? Just a bed seeming to be the only comfort. What did I do? What did we do? Us all together, strangers but yet very similar. Secluded, alone, locked up. Of what sin did we do—a hospital?

—Steve Girten, 2009

The encounter that people think is love. With the excitement of being with others and of what fun that may occur! When wondering of our feelings and reflecting back on them, we may remain content. But love itself is different. Love basically is a feeling of being close and trusted and a happiness of shared openness, interest. Love can never truly be expected. So you smile and see of the love that is waiting.

—Steve Girten, May 11, 2012

"The Shaman"

Mystical leader, carry us with your powers, with all the energies of the universe—the sun, the sky of intrigue, the glowing moon, and the living of all entities. The truths of knowledge and the awareness of our abilities. A journey through aspects of our dreams with the idea of enlightenment of wisdom to gain.

"Energies of the Universe"

Harmony

—Steve Girten, May 9, 2012

To reach out and touch that hand near the top of that mountain. And to realize that brotherhood is never forgotten.

—Steve Girten, April 18, 2012

The beauty of nature is given with free love. Aspects of our soul, defying creativity. I love the scent of the fresh air.

—Steve Girten, April 27, 2012

The pride of the American way. With a perception as clear as our reality. The sanction of structured freedom—beautiful! With people who care for the land of the free and home of the brave. Prove your love and to be what you want to be.

—Steve Girten, May 3, 2012

Born with a special mind and have died in so many ways. The gift of love that slows me down. The wisdom I receive with tears in my eyes.

—Steve Girten, May 7, 2012

"Reality"

The fear of reality, the people who share the go between the surroundings of circumstances of spontaneous natures. Feelings, reactions. But we all touch base with reality—good or bad. But it does help us deal with our feeling that becomes too much.

True reality is just a blur that we hardly notice.

—Steve Girten, Date Unknown

The mind and its power, our love, and the universe. And where is our location of destiny, and where is it longing to be? So just smile for me, and your bright eyes, let them shine. With this wonderful being of life that you are. Feeling you so close, my imagination, it flows. With a power of compassion that is very similar to love. Just the touch of your skin, the incredible sense it brings.

—Steve Girten, January 27, 2012

As love being the first cause of religion and a way to follow. But lust was there as well with intentions, which only lead to greed and hatred. Oh, the sins that came.

—Steve Girten, March 26, 2012

As our worries lie dormant with little to say. And the dreams that slip away one by one. With the world dark and scary and no love around. And of the government that controls a sanction power of laws in all our lives to follow.

—Steve Girten, April 12, 2012

The fall of an empire, what is remembered of this history? The history of the lament, the power, and the lives of societies. The governments of greed. Just to view the past with intelligence and intrigue. And of what really went wrong? But to also learn by looking back at the past, the failures, and the incomplete attempts. We should learn to live and live to learn.

—Steve Girten, March 5, 2012

The perfection of life that leads to immortality.

—Steve Girten, February 21, 2012

I live and I learn to grow is always possible. At the darkest nights and at the saddest moments, alone is never really true. Your heart that pumps and is felt, is your faith, and of body and the mind as one. Like the soul that brings awareness to the being you are.

—Steve Girten, March 2, 2012

Feeling your love and to know your love. Please help me find myself and to focus and keep your life with me. I love you, but so lost I get, so misled. And trying to remember the special way you are, and what you mean to me, and how life is fulfilled and to be happy of us together. My dear, through the world's difficulties and the pain of others in life. We do still remain together as one. Stay with me.

—Steve Girten, February 21, 2012

Man and spirit, existence and being. Our soul and immortality. With our body being a substance, and the brain's function that of chemistry, and all the internal organs that keep the body flow. Our image, appearance, the skin that's wrapped around our body of bones, the incredible structure of the human figure. We are just mere objects being observed from a far. But we must cheat, trick to beat the loss of feelings, to satisfy comfort, and to attain. The deep greed that lurks in any person. Being right, being true, trying to do everything right, to be your best of ability in anything that you do. But to also understand your limits and also follow your dreams, of passions that are endless. Just your formation, your soul glowing, and of all reflected love.

—Steve Girten, Date Unknown

The night is dark, and the air is felt around. As the wheels roll, crowded is the street. Beams of light from objects that surround. Shall the sun rise and change this distorted vision of an illusion of life seen? A feeling of detachment and of withdrawn from the world.

—Steve Girten, March 1, 2012

So little but so much, I give my life for cause to influence a movement of love and/or brotherhood. The struggle of self-want and the external interference that holds me back, but with my power of confidence and of compassion, I will find an answer.

—Steve Girten, February 7, 2012

In the labyrinth of life, we walk through traditions of past worlds. The passages of the ages, just being so free and with amazement we see. With the eyes seeing the sun and as we have just begun. But the pain, like a knife stabbed in our side. Announcing the gods to stand alone, to rise above. For our quest of knowledge and of knowing, to seek for the sky, to give us answers to set us free. "For someone who's so unknown yet *adored*."

—Steve Girten, February 1, 2012

In a lucid state, ironic suggestions.

I love your eyes, smile as I feel your thighs.

The dark brings secrets to the night.

The walk through life and the jog of mainstream, and with a pace sure and confident, we do carry on. Brave are those with cool thoughts in their being of life. And a glimpse of heaven they strive. Their eyes stay bright; their love brings the night. Such as babies that don't know and the old that knows too much.

—Steve Girten, February 7, 2012

Wisdom of the soul, experience of scars through love. To capture the moment of fond memories and smile with the breeze and not worry of your behind and walk forward, proud and sure. And with the sun, a main light to follow. With universal confidence, the gods that watch after all. With a guide following to the processed passion that they live. Existence as the known realms. The mystery of a child who passes unknown time. Where is he? Do I remember any of his daily ways? My son, my daughter, but my life, my job, and my relationships, business, money—of comfort, bills, and checks; but the fear of financial loss, the fear of health problems, and the fear of any close death in my life. Thoughts of society—conformation, the pace, the location at being, where you are really at, and who you are around. With all your dreams, dreams that you should never have to lose. With all your achievements that you should be proud of and to really accept and beat all the harm and sadness that this place Earth brings. Love is forever, but we seldomly notice.

—Steve Girten

Teachers in schools, politicians who rule, cops who enforce the laws. And religion of belief and freedom of life. People who run, people who walk. And the yells, the touch, and the soft tear. So much life and freedom and so much hate and boredom. And not enough awakening to happiness. Is it pain the answer or just waiting for cancer? Is it beer and drugs, or where we came from? Is love dumb or really real to care just to beat any scare?

—Steve Girten, Date Unknown

Distance reasons—ancient voices heard. Alone, no one near, except a dream of your face. You girl, it's you, girl. Everything is you, girl. With the wisdom of God and the curiosity of a child, I see your life as your eyes are seeming to tell.

Your eyes so beautiful and bright, your lips so moist and tight. I hear your name from a far, and I smile and feel dumb.

—Steve Girten, Date Unknown

Structures in difference—watching the world, wondering why. Seeing you and knowing you, meeting, remembering, "touching you." Like the times of our lives, like the tears we cried. Thinking, caring of the past things that were said, arguments that we had. Memories that won't go away! The love I give, and the love that you gave, as much as a heartbeat, as sacred as breath. The dreams of you still last as real as your perfume scent.

—Steve Girten, Date Unknown

The intense feeling of sensuous sex, the curve, the shyness and guilt that is felt from your thigh, your lips that await. Your eyes give me your timing of want, which is to be when we feel the love for each other. With patience and trust and a very deep acceptance of love.

Nature still, a clam breeze, leaves falling in the sun. The dreams that help keep us alive. With a smile for a while. And like the kiss that helps you and me to remember.

—Steve Girten, Date Unknown

Now leaving my home after being there for five years, the loss of a job and a program hopefully for just a short time. Changing my life at a hospital, so it won't be the same as my next home. Adapting once again to strangers and a hope that turns to fear. Worried about life and how to live and feelings that were unlike myself. As I'm looking toward a new home and the past that will go. Satisfaction is needed more than ever, hope that stays but quickly goes away. Wanting freedom, seeking for happiness, but being misunderstood is a daily situation "actions and words." Knowing ambiance of life and what can happen. The shock of love that is real and even any good mood. Feeling now so much older, a young body and an aging head. The mood of sadness and the tears of being so alone and the love that only hurts.

—Steve Girten, 2000

Like in a jail, the time passes. Freedom is too hard to remember. The water and some cigarettes, little food, cups of coffee. And a bed for the head and some clothes I still have and the love I have for you as I sit alone. Wondering for a future, knowing hope. But destiny so impossible. Day by day, life changes; night by night, I live, being right like our love. Together, we're close, as close as two can be. Moon and me, the sight so free, finding the habit of washing like a man, forgetting the cleaning of the street. Interested in learning there are always ways. I do it in my own time, my own style, and yes, in my own way. Busses and jail, on wheels, no secrets and closed in with strangers. Walking on the street, missing your voice. Hey, love you, have you seen her, have you seen her?

—Steve Girten, Date Unknown

The acquired time of the mind—when things slow down, more frequent the clouds that unusually match the night. With a mood of hope but majority vote, so we can cope. A light cigarette and a drink, the wind blows in quest of jet stream, to sink into a chair with you, to share talk and listen to the air. Changes in time the breeze in the air with having thoughts caring and fair.

—Steve Girten, July 21, 2000

Past, past. Low the dark light passes from me. Fear and sad, tears that went. Work friends, friends, the street, the street. Gone now life to live. Did I care? Do I care? I do. Went as she goes. I know, gone, left, and will be no more. As I still see and hear and praying for a soft breeze or rain to save my soul.

The heart that pumps, the lungs that breathe, but the air weakens, and the clouds are waiting above.

—Steve Girten, Date Unknown

"A Good Experience"

Moving to a new place and expecting a better change in my life. And it worked! Feeling free again, with new people and structure, a whole change and chance in life. Sort of like a marriage. Habits of change, to rearrange and not to complain because I am not the same. And less the pain, even from those who complain. Now moving, progressing, matching in all new ways. The faces are new; the talk is the same. Happy now, warm with love, and the hope to awake after sleep. To learn names and actually have the same with my name.

—Steve Girten, Date Unknown

Everyone killing, the world dying. A smile still remains of love and of words that are still heard.

"A world killing is a world dying."

Angel in reflection, sun beam off a car, another cigarette. Patterns of day and of night. Habit of life and of death. Motions of spirits, knowledge of patience, and tricks that lie.

—Steve Girten, Date Unknown

The shrine of life and a celebration of happiness.

The invisible air is gold for us to share.

Unknowledgeable—cause of being to be. Created and uncreated. To exist to discover and feel human. A civilization, a way. Costume to change the flow and a movement that stands for all.

—Steve Girten, Date Unknown

A beam of light pierced through my window.

One morning I awoke with the coffee pot steaming in the kitchen and my radio still playing music from a battery. Just out of the shower, my doorbell rang. I put on my shoes, and then suddenly, a piercing light shone through my room. At first, I jumped, and then I ran from the light, and I just remembered the door. Well, it was my landlord, and he told I need to pay for my electrical bill.

—Steve Girten, Date Unknown

I write simple but with great meaning. From the understandings of inner life/outer life. From the meanings of societies, nations, their beliefs, and all the laws that need to be enforced. The ancient that we reflect back on with some amazement. The stories and the lessons. With the trees and the seas, oh, how we believe. The beautiful air, cold or warm, all around. Just to find that perfect breeze in the summer day or night. To witness the sky of a vast portray of love. As our perception when looking up, it may be distorted, only seeing of what imagination that we have at that time. But such feelings of all sight, feelings of love, hate, and all the sound that is heard. This is all infinite such as our very life.

—Steve Girten, May 7, 2017

From a young age being brought up to be respectful, honest, trustworthy, and caring. Through the years, I have really learned to be sympathetic to all I see and feel. This I realize now at about forty-nine years old and that what I have learned can lead me to a great meaning of my life. Awareness of intrigue, spiritual wisdom, belief and pride, an enlightenment of knowledge, and a compassion of being. "To really live!"

—Steve Girten, December 6, 2016

As we go through life, we will have some kind of feeling to care, to give as much as we can, to find compassion in our heart. And to understand that all our hearts are connected with a flow of love. A divine nature of sharing love! That of universal love or that of God. The beauty of the awakening from the within and of the without—*peace will come.* Every moment has significance, with the goal for perfection that becomes a divine entity in awareness.

—Steve Girten, December 14, 2016

As the dark came and with it the rain. Darkness, darkness, as the sky itself opens and its white bolt of lightning strikes across the very sight of our sky. As the eyes that look above and with the rain we feel. Dismal, damp, and a power that seems to want to take over. All this as if an ancient battle is going on, with the power of genres of rulers—gods, all past deities, queens, pharaohs, kings. But on Earth the control of land, slaves they were, so sad they are lives forgotten. But the love of sacred power from our heavens and from our traveled planet that we exist on.

—Steve Girten, June 19, 2017

The power of the mind, patterns in time, of thoughts and power of memory. Blowing in the wind, our heads fill the sky. Forever the love lasts. To be free, unemotional moments of freedom. But the optimistic eyes that seem to smile and with a tear caused from all the negative feelings from strangers. Oh, the hurt of love. And the disappointment with struggle and of what gain. With a reasoning to accept but with nothing to compare with.

—Steve Girten, 2007

To see, to feel, to be free of reality in reality. Friends and friends, drink and drink, love and adore the signs. Cocaine stops the pain, and then you feel the same.

Opposite ways for a new life to match. People go on with the scar of life, love, hate, attempts, accomplishments, reward, and sacrifice but to keep trying and never really give up. What you know is yours to treasure or to bury it. The innate feel of life with life itself going on without end.

—Steve Girten

A choice for a new and better breed, with progression the way of the world. The believer of freedom and broke through all the greed.

Beyond betrayal, the eyes of the believer.

Awkward—awakening of all emotions in freedom, just to feel. The effort of our ego, so elegant, embracing the souls of realm's all around.

—Steve Girten, October 18, 2016

The burden of boredom, the smiles are few.

Blameless of her, so carefree with her love so deep inside.

—Steve Girten, October 18, 2016

"Enlightened by a Light"

Our appearance is our inner power.

Our compassion is our peace inside.

Love is in you, not without you.

> —Steve Girten, October 24, 2016

The wisdom of the worldly, seeking new knowledge, perfection in a world, and eager with satisfaction. Wanting celebration of existence with description of all endeavors given and all who endure the pain of the true earth. The essence of equality, the esteem of respect, and the compassion of our fellowmen.

> —Steve Girten, October 24, 2016

The power of the sun, the light is endless. In regard to the experience of sun, it might not be alone. The complexity of existence. Absorbs, filters through our very life. This brings forth the ideas of blood and water that flows in us. Even the sky so vast and cool has surrendered to interference of universal laws. The light we can see, but the power is something we actually feel.

> —Steve Girten, January 30, 2007

"Healing"

Is it our head, or is it our pain, how we feel, or the same? The hurt from within, the struggle of survival, and the pain that just doesn't go away, the effort to achieve, to be more, and the want that turns to greed. The fear that which holds us back when we're so near. What keeps us right? Is it the urge to progress, or is it the feeling of giving up? Is it our head, or is it our pain to be dead, or is it the same?

—Steve Girten, 2007

Realms of ancient life. The past and what did last. Books of histories, sculptures, artifacts, the words of belief. Power, gold and control, and the many true accounts of their culture. And of their dreams that keep and have kept us wondering. Their power with struggles, force, and patience in matching of a divine way. Without understanding of hurt, love, and human. "Ancient Egypt."

—Steve Girten, 2007

Adhering to the feelings to follow my soul for wisdom.

From the betrayal of awakened scars that caused the burden of the giving and of the living and of all the loss of responsibilities that become.

To capture the "sun dance" in full chance. The charm of a young child feels the beads that are dangling from your hair that flows. The eyes that shine and the love that grows.

—Steve Girten, 2007

Seeing the sky is like imagining the sky with the clouds, clouds way up high. This brings enlightenment; this brings a feeling of content, a feeling of peace, a feeling of sorrow. But just to remember of any of fear, love will always be near.

—Steve Girten, 2007

The birth of love and religion of freedom.

—Steve Girten, 2007

www.ingramcontent.com/pod-product-compliance
Lightning Source LLC
Chambersburg PA
CBHW051449250726
48655CB00001B/327